Contents

4

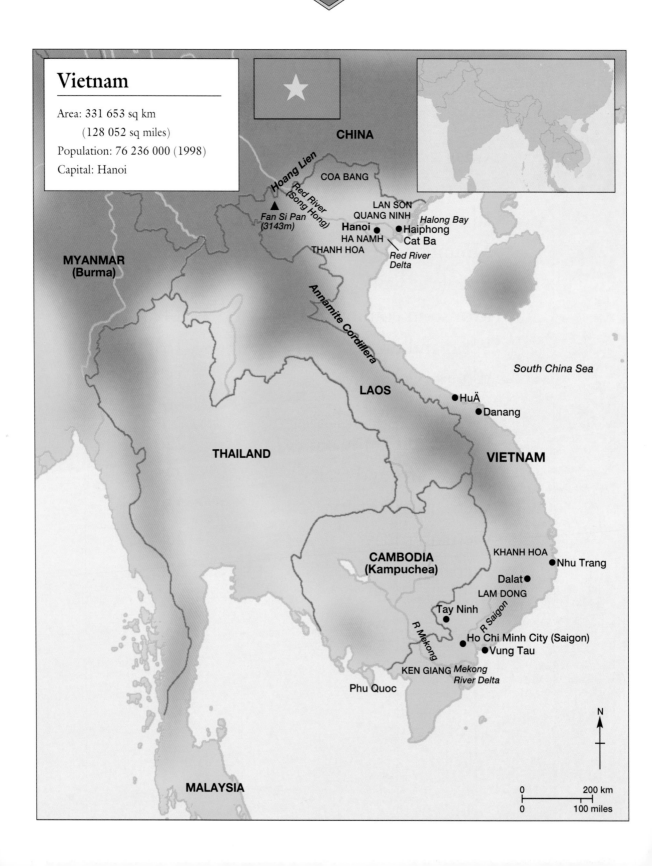

Vietnam

Area: 331 653 sq km
(128 052 sq miles)
Population: 76 236 000 (1998)
Capital: Hanoi

CHINA

COA BANG

Hoang Lien

LAN SON
QUANG NINH

Red River
(Song Hong)

Halong Bay

▲
Fan Si Pan
(3143m)

Hanoi ● ● Haiphong
HA NAMH   Cat Ba
THANH HOA
Red River
Delta

MYANMAR
(Burma)

Annamite Cordillera

LAOS

South China Sea

● HuÄ
● Danang

THAILAND

VIETNAM

CAMBODIA
(Kampuchea)

KHANH HOA
● Nhu Trang

Dalat ●

LAM DONG

Tay Ninh
●

R Saigon

R Mekong

● Ho Chi Minh City (Saigon)
● Vung Tau

KEN GIANG Mekong
River Delta

Phu Quoc

MALAYSIA

N

0   200 km

0   100 miles

DISCOVERING

◆

VIETNAM

By Richard Balkwill

A ZOË BOOK

A ZOË BOOK

© 2000 Zoë Books Limited

Devised and produced by
Zoë Books Limited
15 Worthy Lane
Winchester
Hampshire SO23 7AB
England

First published in Great Britain in 2000 by
Zoë Books Limited
15 Worthy Lane
Winchester
Hampshire SO23 7AB

A record of the CIP data is available from the
British Library.

ISBN 1 874488 93 2

Printed in Hong Kong by Midas Printing Ltd.
Design: Sterling Associates
Map: Sterling Associates
Production: Grahame Griffiths

Photographic acknowledgments

The publishers wish to acknowledge, with thanks,
the following photographic sources:

Cover: Impact Photos/Mark Henley; Title page
Hutchison Picture Library/Nigel Sitwell; 5r TRIP/J
Sweeney, 5b TRIP/T Bognar; 6 Hutchison Picture
Library/Jeremy Horner; 7l Impact Photos/Mark
Henley, 7r Impact Photos/Nigel Amies; 8 Impact
Photos/Alain Evrard; 9l TRIP/R Nichols, 9r TRIP/
A Ghazzal; 10 TRIP/T Bognar; 11l Hutchison
Picture Library/Jeremy Horner; 11r Impact Photos/
Colin Jones; 12 Hutchison Picture Library/Sarah
Errington; 13l Impact Photos/Colin Jones, 13r
Impact Photos/Stefan Boness; 14 Impact Photos/
Simon Cooper; 15l Impact Photos/Andy Soloman;
15r TRIP/J Sweeney; 16 Impact Photos/Alain
Evrard; 17l Hutchison Picture Library/Timothy
Beddow; 17r Impact Photos/Alain Evrard; 18
TRIP/A Ghazzal; 19l Hutchison Picture Library/
Robert Francis; 19r TRIP/B Vikander; 20 & 21l
Hutchison Picture Library/Sarah Murray; 21r Impact
Photos/Mark Henley; 22 Hutchison Picture
Library/Jeremy Horner; 23l TRIP/A Tovy; 23r
Hutchison Picture Library/John Hatt; 24 TRIP/
Viesti Associates; 25l Impact Photos/Charles Coates,
25r Impact Photos/Daniel White; 26 Impact
Photos/Mark Henley; 27l Hutchison Picture Library;
27r Impact Photos/Colin Jones; 28 TRIP/A
Ghazzal; 29l Hutchison Picture Library/Sarah
Murray; 29r TRIP/A Tovy.

The publishers have made every effort to trace the
copyright holders, but if they have inadvertently
overlooked any, they will be pleased to make the
necessary arrangement at the first opportunity

Cover: *Working in the rice fields in the
Mekong Delta*

Title page: *A monk in the Minh Trang pagoda*

Chào dón!

Welcome to Vietnam! The map of Vietnam shows why some people thought the country was like the legendary dragon fish. The tail spreads out in the north and the body curves down to the head and snout at the south western tip.

This S-shaped land has 3600 km (2250 miles) of coastline. It borders China, Laos and Cambodia. Much of the country is hilly and mountainous, including the Annamite range to the west. Vietnam's highest mountain is Fan Si Pan in the Hoang Lien range in the northwest. It is 3143 metres (10 312 feet) high. Farmers grow rice, coffee, tea and rubber in the Mekong River Delta in the south and the Red River Delta in the north.

Since 1940, there have been many wars in Vietnam. At different times, France, the United States of America (USA) and China have all been involved. From 1954 to 1975, Vietnam

Farmers carrying rice plants

was divided into two countries, North Vietnam and South Vietnam. Now, in peacetime, the reunited country is called the Socialist Republic of Vietnam. Most people still work in fishing or agriculture, although the country is building up industry and trade with other parts of the world. Tourists are again visiting the country's beautiful cities and countryside.

Fishing at dawn, Halong Bay

Rivers of the south - Nam Bo

The waterfront on the Saigon River, Ho Chi Minh City

There are three different regions in Vietnam. The south is called Nam Bo. Its main city was once called Saigon. Saigon has been renamed Ho Chi Minh City after the leader who inspired the people from 1945 until his death in 1989. It is the largest city in the country.

Ho Chi Minh City is full of cyclists and motorcyclists. Not many ordinary Vietnamese people have cars. Crowds of workers, street market stall holders, students and tourists make the city lively and colourful.

The River Saigon flows through Ho Chi Minh City on its way to the South China Sea. At the popular

Women in a bicycle taxi

resort of Vung Tau, visitors enjoy fine beaches and clean water. More than half the people in the country follow the Buddhist religion and there are many shrines and statues in Vung Tau, including a 12 metre (40feet) Buddha and a brass bell weighing 5000 kg (nearly 5 tonnes).

The River Mekong

The great River Mekong, called the 'Mother of Life', flows through the Nam Bo region. The river floods each year during the monsoon season. Beside the river, farmers grow rice in the rich mud and silt which the floodwater carries down. People who live on the river earn their living by fishing.

As the Mekong nears the sea, it splits into a vast delta of more than 3.7 million hectares (about 8 million acres). The local people call it the 'River of Nine Dragons'. Each wetland 'dragon' is a province. The river floods make the land fertile. About 170 years ago, when France ruled the area, canals were dug here and this has helped to improve the land.

If you take a trip on the river you will see huge mangrove trees growing by the water. Bees collect honey from the mangrove blossom. The wetlands are full of wonderful birds, insects and flowers.

'Treasure Island'

In the southwest of Vietnam is the province of Ken Giang, on the Cambodian border. Here there are more than a hundred islands with beautiful mountains, beaches and clear blue seas, full of fish. The land is rich in minerals. The best known island, Phu Quoc, was once called Phu Quy, or 'treasure island'. The 48 km (30 miles) long island is visited mainly by wealthy tourists.

The Qwan Yin statue, Vung Tau

In the middle - the Trung Bo

The Po Nagar Tower ruins, Nhu Trang

The narrow centre of Vietnam is known as the Trung Bo. The old name 'Annam' is still used for the mountains on the west side, the Annamite Cordillera. The mountains were the European sailors' first sight of Vietnam.

Coming up National Highway Number 1 from the south, you come to the province of Khanh Hoa, called the 'sandal province' after the sandalwood trees which grow here. The hard, sweet-smelling wood is used to build houses and furniture.

Nhu Trang is the capital of the province. It is a favourite coastal resort.

Above the city stands a huge, white stone Buddha, 14 metres (46 feet) high. Here you can taste the famous pink *thanh long*, or 'green dragon fruit', which is delicious to eat or to make into a drink.

The province of Lam Dong lies inland in the central highland region. This area is more than 900 metres (2952 feet) above sea level. Tea and coffee are grown here. The ancient, hill-top capital of Dalat was once known as 'Le Petit Paris'. Tourists love to visit this beautiful town. They can buy *dau hu* here - a milk pudding sold by women who carry it in a bowl at the end of a bamboo pole.

Around HuÄ

The old capital of the central region was HuÄ, on the River Huong Giang. Near HuÄ is the demilitarised zone – the DMZ – which marked the boundary between North and South Vietnam from 1945 until 1975.

This area was once part of the ancient Southern Kingdom. Ruins of temples and sanctuaries still stand, such as the beautiful, 600-year-old tower of Po Klong Garai. The Merian festival at

The beach, Nhu Trang

The Imperial City, HuÄ

Ponaja Cham Towers takes place on the Cai River in Nhu Trang. The Cham people lived here for hundreds of years.

Today, the most important town is Danang, on the River Hau. Danang is a port and an industrial centre. The nearby country of Laos, which has no coastline, also exports goods from Danang. Danang has fine beaches. There are sometimes surfing competitions here. People harvest raffia, catch fish or make salt.

After the last war ended in 1975, trees were needed to replace those which had been destroyed. The Bai Cat Tien National Park is a nursery for this replanting programme.

The Marble Mountains

Inland from Danang are the five Marble Mountains, named after the basic elements – water, wood, gold, fire and earth. The highest peak, Thuy Son, looks like an egg which has been cracked open. Children earn money by guiding visitors to the natural caves. There are sand martins' nests in the caves and cliffs here.

Mountains of the north – Bac Bo

Boats on the Red River, near Hanoi

The Bac Bo region in the north is mountainous. Most people here live in the country's capital, Hanoi, and the main port of Haiphong. The peoples of Tonkin, as this area was called, have lived here for more than 2000 years.

The climate is cooler here, and in the mountains around Hanoi there is a winter season. Hill peoples such as the Black Tai and the Muong live in the far north. The Muong people have no written language. In the Lang Son province, roads are bad and people have to travel in jeeps or buses. Journeys are very slow. The Pu Peo, Lodo, and Phu La people live in the northern parts of Vietnam. They have their own customs, with elaborate marriage and burial ceremonies.

The mountains contain valuable minerals such as silver and zinc. Cotton, tea, and flowers grow well in the cool climate. Flowers are grown here for the bees to produce honey. In Cao Bang province, the Ba Be Lakes area is full of rivers, valleys, lakes and caves.

In the Ha Namh province you can visit Cu Phuong National Park. Here there are deep caves, tall trees, creepers, orchids and camellias. Monkeys and gibbons live in the trees, and there are exotic birds and flying lizards. Many other wild animals and rare snakes live in this remote paradise.

Harvesting tea

Red River

The Red River – *Song Hong* – flows through the middle of the northern part of the country. Its name comes from the coloured sand and mud which the river floods bring down from the mountains.

The capital, Hanoi, stands on the Red River. The city is smaller than Ho Chi Minh City. Its museum commemorates Ho Chi Minh, the founder of modern Vietnam. Nearby is the Thanh Hoa province, where the ancient Le people lived. The farmers in this area have found a kind of rice which will grow in the salty ground.

To the east lies Haiphong, on the River Cam. This industrial centre is Vietnam's third largest city. Factories employ workers to make cement, build ships and can foods. Nearby Quang Ninh province is Vietnam's main coal-mining area.

Cat Ba National Park

People from Hanoi and Haiphong often travel to the Cat Ba National Park. It is an island with coral reefs, turtles, and oyster and conch shells.

Halong Bay is filled with thousands of beautiful, tiny islands. Halong means 'where the dragon descends into the sea'. A legend tells how a great dragon came down from the mountains to the sea. Lashing its tail, it dug out valleys and hollows in the ground. When the dragon jumped into the sea, the water rose. It filled the hollows and valleys, and left islands in the water.

Some local people believe that a sea monster known as the *Tarasque* haunts the waters round Halong Bay.

Boats in Halong Bay

People at work

Fishing on a lake near Ho Chi Minh City

More than two-thirds of adults in Vietnam work in agriculture. The main crop is rice, which grows under water in irrigated fields, or as a dry crop. Other food crops include sugar cane, maize and potatoes.

Very few farmers have machinery to help them to work the land. Sometimes they put piles of rice stalks beside the road to dry. Then they spread them on the road. Passing cars and trucks drive over the stalks and separate the grain from them.

In cooler mountain regions, people work on tea and coffee plantations. Rubber trees have been planted, and tobacco is grown. Hardwoods such as mahogany and sandalwood are valuable exports. However, many trees were destroyed in wars and it is taking a long time to grow them again. Mulberry bushes provide food for silkworms.

Fishing

Vietnam's coastline is more than 2500 kilometres (1560 miles) long. Many people who live near the sea or the river estuaries work at fishing or in the fishing industry. Other people work in fish processing plants, making the smelly, fermented sauce known as *nuoc mam*.

Gathering rice

Natural resources

Vietnam has many natural resources. Minerals such as oil and bauxite could make the country a major producer of its own petrol and aluminium. Other valuable minerals include silver, copper and antimony. However, at the moment there are few mines.

Roads are bad and it is difficult to transport raw materials or to build factories away from the few big cities. Every bridge in North Vietnam had to be rebuilt after the war. For many years, Vietnam exported scrap steel and brass, mainly to Japan. Crashed aircraft and abandoned weapons provided metal to make bicycles and motorcycles.

Growing trade

After the country was reunited in 1975, Vietnam traded a great deal with Russia. Vietnam exported wood, sugar and oil, and imported machinery. However, they paid much more for their imports than they received from the goods they sold to other countries. Many of the products made in Vietnam were not of good enough quality to sell outside the country.

Things are changing at last for the people of Vietnam. Trade with other countries is growing fast. Tourists are coming to the country in large numbers, and hotels are being built. Until 1994, Vietnam did not trade with the United States. Today, American advisers are helping to build offices, factories, hospitals and schools. Industry is expanding, and trade with China is growing too.

At work in a metal factory

Monsoon country

Terraced fields cleared in the mountain forests, northern Vietnam

The weather in Vietnam varies a lot. The climate is generally very different between north and south. The south is near the Equator, and has a tropical climate. Strong winds, or monsoons, bring rain. Hot, wet weather from May to September makes the country very green and fertile. It is much drier in winter.

In the north, the weather is cooler. In Hanoi, it can get quite cold (5°C/40°F), and in the mountains there are frosts in January. Typhoons can hit the east coast of Vietnam in August and September. These violent, hurricane-force winds bring torrential rains which destroy buildings and crops. At other times, damp fogs bring fine drizzle known as the *crachin* (from the French *cracher*, 'to spit'). Vietnamese people call this 'flying rain'.

Plants grow easily and quickly in the warm, wet climate, and there is usually a second crop of rice in February or March. Much of the country used to be covered in thick forest, but chemicals were used in the war to destroy the leaves of trees where soldiers might be hiding, and petrol in jelly (napalm) was dropped to burn down trees. Mountain people cut down trees for firewood and to clear space to grow crops. Hardwoods are also cut down and exported. In 1983, only 24 per cent of the forest cover was left.

Wildlife

In wartime, polluted water and chemicals killed off many wild creatures. However, there are now 750 species of bird in Vietnam. Rare kingfishers and hornbills live beside water or in trees. Insects, including tropical butterflies, are common again. Bees are attracted by flowers, and honey is made and exported. Flowers are sold in many street markets. There are different kinds of orchid, such as the beautiful coral

A colourful butterfly

Frog Lake, Cat Ba Island National Park

and the vanilla orchids. Others look like a butterfly in flight.

Places like the Cuc Phuong National Park are home to a huge variety of wildlife. Mammals such as elephants, monkeys and black bears can still be found, although tigers and panthers are now very rare. Some species, such as the tapir, are extinct and many species are threatened, including the kouprey (a kind of ox) and the rhinoceros. In warmer areas, snakes such as the boa constrictor and the small, poisonous krait can be found. Flying lizards are common, too.

Plans to enlarge national parks and replant forests will help to make sure that Vietnam saves its plant life and its wildlife.

Food and drink

A display of pomelo fruit at a market

Some people say there are as many as 500 local dishes in Vietnam! Many people eat while on the move. Travelling to work, they may stop for breakfast at a *Com Pho* stall. *Pho* is 'fast food', made of rice or noodles with minced pork or chicken, onions, vegetables and ginger. It is served with fresh herbs and the fish sauce called *nuoc mam*. Monosodium glutamate (msg) adds flavour to some dishes. The white crystals you see in a dish on the table will be msg, not salt or sugar!

At mealtimes, Vietnamese families serve themselves with rice from a shared rice bowl. They add meat, fish or vegetables, and eat the mixture with chopsticks. Soups are popular, and people eat spring rolls, *cha gio*, as a snack. Rice paper is rolled round minced pork, onions and mushrooms, then deep fried. Many people follow the Buddhist faith and eat only vegetarian foods.

Special foods

Swallow nest soup is a speciality, and restaurants also serve frogs, snails, snakes, bats and porcupines. Children eat simpler foods, such as *banh cuom*, a rice pancake made with pork, spices and fresh herbs. They do not usually eat western snacks such as hamburgers or potato chips.

Cooking hot snacks

Fruit and drinks

Vegetables and fruit grow well in Vietnam's climate. Coconuts are very popular, and the milk is a favourite drink. Oranges, lemons and melons grow in many places. Local fruits include rombutan, lychee, and durian (which smells bad but tastes good!)

Vietnamese children like sweet things, including ice cream (known as *kem*) or frozen yoghurt. Traditional desserts are made with rice flour. A soft, sticky mixture of rice, beans and sugar, called *banh it nhan dau*, is steamed and served in a folded banana leaf. Sweet and savoury foods are often mixed. You may be given avocado pears with ice and sugar, or a rice cake, *banh chung*, containing dried fruit, meat and onions.

Sweet, fizzy drinks are made from fruit such as guavas and lychees. Lemon soda (*so-da chanh*) is another refreshing drink. Coffee and tea are grown in Vietnam, and served hot or cold. Local beer, known as *Ba muoi bia* or '33 beer', can quench your thirst on a hot day, but rice wine (*ruou*) is used for cooking rather than drinking. Trade with Russia in the 1980s means that vodka is sometimes drunk. It is a strong, expensive spirit. Many people also chew betel nuts for refreshment. The nuts make a red juice which stains your teeth brown!

A boy selling sweet cakes

Where people live

Most people in Vietnam live in cities such as Ho Chi Minh City and Hanoi, or in the fertile valleys of the Mekong and Red River deltas. In the hills and mountains to the west and north of the country, many different peoples live a simple village life that has been unchanged for many years.

People often move to the cities to find work. In Ho Chi Minh City and Hanoi, housing is a problem. Families sometimes live in very poor, crowded conditions, without electricity or running water.

Chinese people have lived in Vietnam for thousands of years. Most cities have a Chinese district. In the 'Cholon' area of Ho Chi Minh City, markets open early and close late, and are full of noise and colour. However, workers and travellers can find a quiet place for prayer and thought in the many temples.

In the river valleys, families live near or on the water. Fishing people live and work in boats, or build houses over the water. Typhoons bring heavy rain and violent winds which can damage or destroy these homes.

For many Vietnamese people, the direction in which their doors and windows face is very important. This is called geomancy. Geomancers advise people how to place and build their houses.

Modern flats above shops on a main road, Ho Chi Minh City

Shacks by the River Saigon

At home

Most Vietnamese houses are built of hardwood, such as sandalwood. They are decorated with beautifully carved animals to bring good fortune or protection from evil spirits. The tortoise and the phoenix are symbols of long life. The dragon brings wisdom and knowledge.

In some small towns and villages you will see communal houses or *dinh*. Their roofs stand on columns, and there are nine rooms inside. The rooms are linked so that people can meet and talk together, or have some privacy. Outside, the edges of the roofs curl up to allow light and air to come in. This also helps to keep the house warm in winter and cool in summer.

In the mountains and the remote north country, Muong and Thai peoples build wooden or bamboo houses on stilts. Bamboo curtains divide the rooms, and an open fire burns for cooking.

The kitchen is at the centre of most Vietnamese houses. Cooking is done on charcoal over a small clay stove. Food is usually grilled and kept hot at the table on another stove. Families often eat food with their right hand.

Most houses in Vietnam have an altar. Vietnamese people believe that when a member of their family dies, he or she continues to guide and protect those still living.

An altar at home

The 'big cities'

The Huc (Rising Sun) bridge over Hoan Kiem Lake, Hanoi

Hanoi, the capital of Vietnam, is a city of about one million people. It stands on the Red River, where the emperor of the Ly dynasty established it in AD1010. A story tells that he saw a flying dragon which lit up the sky, and built the capital of his empire where he saw this *thang long*, 'soaring dragon'. A district of Hanoi is still called Thang Long.

The city's name was once Dong Kinh ('Eastern Capital'). It has been known as Hanoi ('City on a bend in the river') since 1831. Unlike many big cities, the noise in Hanoi is not the roar of cars, buses and trucks. Most people ride bicycles or motorcycles, or take tram cars which rattle, clang, and squeal round sharp corners. There are also bicycle taxis, or cyclos.

Hanoi has parks and lakes, with trees and beautiful pagodas. Hoan Kiem Lake is in the middle of the city. Its name means 'restored sword'. A legend tells how, 500 years ago, an emperor was given a magical sword to drive the Chinese out of Vietnam. Later, while he was rowing a boat on the lake, a huge turtle took the sword back to the depths of the lake. Today, people get up early to jog round the lake or take exercise before going to work.

The Dong Xuan market sells all kinds of fruit and vegetables, and medicines made from the venom found in snakes. Much of Hanoi is still very poor. It is crowded and there is no water or electricity. Many new buildings are now being built.

Praying at a shrine, Hanoi

Ho Chi Minh City

Ho Chi Minh City, once known as Saigon, is a much bigger place than Hanoi, with nearly 4 million inhabitants. The city is alive with people bringing goods to markets, setting up stalls to sell food and all kinds of other products.

Most people travel around on bicycles or motorcycles. A small Japanese motorcycle can cost four times an ordinary person's yearly salary. Some electrical goods are brought in cheaply but are expensive to buy. The sellers and buyers do not pay tax to the government on these items. This 'black market' allows people to add to their low income.

Even teenage children have to work. Some carry tourists and visitors on rickshaws - bicycle taxis. Others come in from the surrounding country bringing animals and birds to sell in the markets. The biggest is the Huynh Thue Khang street market. It sells anything from cassette players to clothing. The Ben Thanh market sells vegetables, fruit and all kinds of food. Some families eat in big food halls, like a school dining room, where food is cheap.

Some buildings date from the time when the French ruled Ho Chi Minh City, after 1859. The Christian cathedral, built in 1883, is called Notre Dame ('Our Lady'), like the much older building in Paris. Pagodas and temples are everywhere, as most people follow the Hindu and Buddhist religions. Down beside the Saigon River is District 4, the poorest part of town. Here, dozens of families live on crowded old sailing boats called junks.

Cholon Market, Ho Chi Minh City

People and language

Many people who live in Vietnam came originally from Indonesia. Today, almost all the people (90 per cent) are Viet people. Away from the big cities, different peoples lead lives which have not changed for thousands of years. Some small groups live in mountains to the west and north of Vietnam. The French called them *montagnards* ('mountain people'), but they are not a single group. There are more than 50 small ethnic, religious or cultural groups.

The largest group is made up of Chinese people. China borders Vietnam and for many years Chinese rulers governed the country. Today, most Chinese live in the big cities.

A Hmong girl in Lao Cai province, close to the Chinese border

Thai and Khmer peoples live in the countryside. Khmer people came from Cambodia. Parts of Cambodia and Vietnam once formed the Champa Kingdom, and you can still see the Cham towers which were once places of worship.

Clothes

In Vietnam's tropical climate, loose clothes and open shoes are best. Most men and women wear a shirt and trousers for work, and for important occasions such as a wedding, they put on a long tunic, or *ao dai*. Everyone

Selling coned hats

wears a coned hat to keep the sun and rain off. People wear sandals made of rubber and plastic, as well as leather.

Religions

People follow many different religions in Vietnam. The main one is Buddhism. Buddhists believe in morality, good will towards all people, contemplation, and virtue. They hope to reach a state of *nirvana* in which they are in perfect peace and harmony with themselves and with others.

Confucianism follows the ideas of the Chinese leader Confucius, who laid down rules about how people should behave towards each other. Obeying rulers and parents, being loyal to friends and educating your children well, are all important to Confucians. Portuguese and French settlers brought Christianity to Vietnam. Roman Catholicism is common in Vietnam. The Catholic churches in big cities were built by the French.

The written word

For many years, China ruled in Vietnam, and the Vietnamese language is written in Chinese characters. Chinese is a pictogram language – the words are shown in pictures. The early Christian missionaries invented *quoc ngu*, which uses Roman letters to write down Vietnamese. However, there are only 26 letters in the Roman alphabet, and Chinese has many more characters. So the same written word in *quoc ngu* means many different things. The word *hai* means 'two' but it also means 'shoe'! The rise and fall of your voice, and accents on the words, are the only ways of telling the difference.

The Great Temple at Tay Ninh near Cambodia

Culture and sports

Dragon dancing at Tet, *the new year festival*

Vietnam celebrates many festivals. *Tet* (in February) is important, marking the beginning of a religious new year, when families remember their ancestors. Children help to decorate the home with peach blossom, and a basket of nuts and bamboo is hung out on the top of a long bamboo pole. This 'signal tree' is meant to keep away evil spirits. If the first person to visit you in the new year is good and kind, it is a good omen.

Music is an important part of life in Vietnam. People sing and play instruments at festivals. Traditional singing, known as *ca tru*, is verse set to music. The story tells of family life, peace and happiness. A traditional instrument is the *thue*, a flute made of bamboo.

Tuong opera is performed by singers who mime the action of a well-known historical event. Their costumes are very bright, and they paint their faces in strong colours.

Children love to watch *roi nuoc*, water puppets, a show which you find only in Vietnam. The people operating the puppets have to work partly under water. They pull or push rods, strings and pulleys to make the puppets move over the surface of the water. Characters such as dragons, fairies or spirits act out well-known stories.

Sports

In school all children are taught gymnastics, and practise hard for displays to their teachers and parents. Many people in Vietnam live near the sea, so water sports are popular, especially swimming and diving.

Today, international sports are played in Vietnam. Soccer is a favourite, as well as wrestling and warlike exercises called martial arts. Pool is also popular. The players aim a stick, or cue, at balls on a cloth-covered board, and try to get them into pockets at the side of the table.

Arts and crafts

Some of the most beautiful works of art in Vietnam, pottery and carvings, are more than a thousand years old. The ancient stone and wood carvings

A water puppet show, Hanoi

Decorating a pagoda

found in Central Vietnam are even older, as are the huge bronze drums for collecting rain, found near Hanoi.

People still make pottery and weave and embroider cloth. Ceramics is the art of coating the surface of a pot or dish with a white clay, and then painting it. White and blue ceramic designs show flowers, birds, and rivers, and scenes from the many festivals.

Lacquerware came originally from China. Teak (a kind of wood) is covered with many coats of the sap from pine trees, or resin, then painted with pictures from ancient myths and legends.

Vietnam in history

China's Han dynasty ruled in Vietnam's Red River Valley area from 111BC. Elsewhere, the Lac Lords ruled. Most people did not own land or houses but lived in a place owned by the lord, who allowed them to grow food as long as they obeyed him. There were rebellions, such as Lady Trien's uprising in AD249, but the Chinese ruled most of Vietnam until 1010, when Ly Cong Van established an independent government. This dynasty ruled for hundreds of years.

From the 1780s, Vietnamese scholars and writers visited Europe, especially France and Portugal. Missionaries from these two countries had brought Roman Catholicism to Vietnam. In 1848, after a revolution in France, French interest in the rich resources of Vietnam increased. From 1859, the French occupied parts of southern Vietnam, and later, Hanoi and HuÄ. The Indo Chinese Union, covering most of modern Vietnam, was established in 1887. Coal, rubber and other valuable resources were exported to France, and French ways of life were imposed on Vietnam.

Vietnamese nationalist groups published books and newspapers opposing French colonial rule. Many of them followed the communist beliefs that all property should be publicly owned, and all actions done for the good of the people.

The City Hall, Ho Chi Minh City was built in the French style.

A temple to Ho Chi Minh

War and peace

During the First World War (1914-18), about 100 000 Vietnamese were sent to fight with the French army. When Nazi Germany invaded France in the Second World War (1940), Germany and Japan were allies (the axis powers). France had to agree to allow Japan to occupy Vietnam. The Viet Minh communists, with help from the American government, tried to force the Japanese out. At the end of the war, the Viet Minh took control of the north, but the French tried to regain control in the south. There was a terrible war from 1946 to 1954, when the French were defeated at the battle of Dien Bien Phu.

An agreement signed in Geneva that year divided the country. A weak, anti-communist leader, Ngo Dinh Diem, ruled the south. In the north, Ho Chi Minh ruled the Democratic Republic of Vietnam, where the Viet Minh (or Viet Cong – short for Vietnam *Cong San*, 'communist') wanted to reunite the country.

In the 1960s, the USA believed that Russian and Chinese communism threatened world peace. They agreed to help South Vietnam against what they saw as a communist threat from the north. The war which followed cost a dreadful amount in lives and money. From 1965 to 1975, about 58 000 Americans were killed, and the war cost the USA $165 billion. The cost to Vietnam was much higher. About 22 000 soldiers in the south and 400 000 in the north died, around four million civilians were killed or injured and the countryside was devastated.

An abandoned US helicopter

Vietnam today

Jeweller's shops lit up at night in Hanoi

After the end of the war in 1975, Vietnam was reunited, but the troubles were not over. The north did not trust the south's loyalty to the new communist rule, and many individuals were persecuted. Then in 1978, a border dispute broke out with Cambodia. While Vietnamese soldiers fought the Khmer Rouge in Cambodia, China attacked Vietnam in support of the Khmer Rouge. This war did not end until 1992, when peace returned to Vietnam after more than 50 years.

Since 1975 the communist government in Vietnam has been helped by the Soviet Union. Russian money was used to help Vietnam rebuild its trade and industry, but progress was very slow. A number of three and five-year plans tried to reform agriculture, fishing and the rebuilding of roads and railways, but trade with Vietnam was very difficult.

For almost 20 years after the American war in Vietnam, the USA did not trade with Vietnam. Americans at that time were still opposed to the communist governments of China and the Soviet Union. But the trade ban, or embargo, was finally lifted by US President Clinton in February 1994. Now American companies are beginning to help to build roads, hospitals and hotels. Trade with other countries is improving.

Building a luxury villa

Towards the future

Vietnam is still a very poor country. Most of the working people make a living from agriculture, growing crops and cultivating small plots of land for themselves and their families. Russian money which was given to Vietnam in the 1980s was meant to build factories and roads, but much of it was spent on setting up the organisations to run the industries. Nearby countries like Thailand and Malaysia were much better at selling what they produced to other countries in the region.

Vietnam has rich and varied raw materials such as wood, rubber, sugar cane and oil. Minerals such as iron ore to make steel, bauxite for aluminium, and precious metals and stones like silver and antimony can all be found in the country, but the equipment to mine these materials is only just beginning to arrive, much of it from Australia. Factories to make tyres and paper, and to refine sugar, are now being built, and oil drilling and refining has begun.

Slowly, the country is beginning to prosper. Firms are now importing parts and assembling electrical goods like radios, hi-fi systems, and televisions, which they can export to other countries.

Hotels are being built and business visitors and tourists are finding it easier to get to and to travel round the country. In 1987, about 20 000 foreigners visited Vietnam. Now the total is expected to be about two million. The door to and from other parts of the world is open at last.

Children in a park in Hanoi

Fact file

Government

The Socialist Republic of Vietnam (*Cong Hoa Xa Hoi Chu Nghia Viet Nam*) has a communist government. The President, *Le Duc Anh*, is Head of State, elected by the National Assembly. He is also a member of the Politburo of the Central Committee. There are about 125 full time members of the Central Committee. The National Assembly (*Quoc Hoi*) has about 500 deputies who each represent 100 000 voters. The 50 provinces have more control of local affairs. These provinces and municipalities are led by officials who are chosen in the area they represent.

Flag

The flag of Vietnam has a yellow star in the middle of a red background. This was the flag of North Vietnam before 1976. The red is for the blood of those who fought for victory, while the gold star is a light to follow for future success and prosperity.

National anthem

This is a battle song called *Tien Quan Ca* ('Marching to the Front').

Religion

About half the population follow either the Buddhist or Confucian religions. Confucians follow another religion whose origin is Chinese. Christianity was introduced from Europe, and about three million people are Roman Catholics. Many families also believe in ancestor worship.

Money

The unit of currency is the dong. More than 10 000 *dong* are equivalent to only one American dollar. The US dollar is also accepted in many places visited by tourists. Most local money is in the form of banknotes from 200 to 10 000 *dong*. There are few coins.

Education

Almost all children in Vietnam receive a primary (elementary) school education from age 6 to 11, but only about 40 per cent go on to secondary or high schools. There are 94 universities, enrolling about 30 000 students every year. Over 80 per cent of the population can read and write.

Newspapers and television

Most of the national newspapers are published in Hanoi, and the content is controlled by the government. *The People* (*Nham Dan*) is the communist party daily newspaper. Business and economic papers like *Vietnam Weekly* are available in English. On the radio, the *Voice of Vietnam* is broadcast in 11 languages. The two television channels broadcast news and information produced by the government.

Some famous people

Hai Ba Trung were three sisters who fought the Chinese and became queens of Vietnam in AD40

Ngo Quyen was the king who in AD938 won independence for Vietnam after 1000 years of Chinese rule

Le Loi was a patriot who fought the Chinese and helped form an independent Vietnam in 1428

Alexandre de Rhodes was the French scholar who, after his first visit to Vietnam in 1627, began to create the *quoc ngu* script

Nguyen Du (1765-1820) was the poet who 'mirrored the hearts, souls and minds' of people in Vietnam

Ho Chi Minh (1890-1969) was the founder of modern Vietnam

Ngoc Van (1906-1954) was a painter who portrayed the struggle against French colonial rule

Huynh Phu So (1919-1947) founded the Hao Buddhist sect in 1939. He cured people miraculously from their diseases. He was assassinated

Tran Luu Han (1920–) is a painter of the resistance who finished the famous 'Hanoi' painting in 1946

Doan Thi Diem (1924–) is a famous poetess and popular folk song writer

Nguyen Van Linh (1930-) was made General Secretary of the Communist Party and is credited with reforms of modern Vietnam

Some key events in history

111BC the Chinese Han dynasty ruled around the Red River valley
AD **44** the Chinese defeated the short rule of the Trung sisters
939 Vietnam became independent from China
1010 the Ly dynasty ruled, and the country became known as Dai Viet
1408 Vietnam again became a province of China
1460-1497 Le Thanh To, leader of the Le dynasty, ruled. He was known as Hong Duc ('Great Virtue').
1874-1887 France gradually gained colonial power over Vietnam
1925 Ho Chi Minh formed a revolutionary youth league against foreign occupation
1940 the Japanese occupied Vietnam
1946-1954 the first Indochina War against the French
1954 Ngo Dinh Diem became first Prime Minister of South Vietnam
1963 Diem was assassinated
1964 The USA began war against North Vietnam
1969 half a million US soldiers were fighting in Vietnam
1973 the peace agreement was signed between the USA and North Vietnam
1975 Saigon fell to the North Vietnamese
1978 the USSR and Vietnam signed a 25-year friendship treaty
1992 the new constitution was established in Vietnam
1994 the USA lifted its economic and trade embargo on Vietnam

Index